help me UNDERSTAND™
Feeling *Regret* & Learning *Wisdom*™

REAL mvpkids®

Ezekiel Builds on his Mistakes

SOPHIA DAY®

Written by Megan Johnson Illustrated by Stephanie Strouse

The Sophia Day® Creative Team-
Stephanie Strouse, Megan Johnson,
Kayla Pearson, Timothy Zowada, Carol Sauder, Mel Sauder

A **special thank you** to our team of reviewers who graciously give us feedback, edits and help ensure that our products remain accurate, applicable and genuinely diverse.

Text and pictures copyrighted © 2019 by MVP Kids Media, LLC

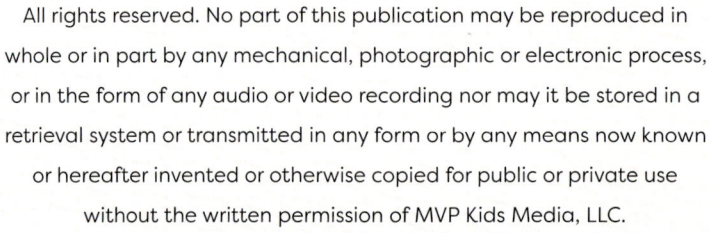

All rights reserved. No part of this publication may be reproduced in whole or in part by any mechanical, photographic or electronic process, or in the form of any audio or video recording nor may it be stored in a retrieval system or transmitted in any form or by any means now known or hereafter invented or otherwise copied for public or private use without the written permission of MVP Kids Media, LLC.

Published and Distributed by MVP Kids Media, LLC - Mesa, Arizona, USA
Printed by RR Donnelley Asia Printing Solutions, Ltd - Dongguan City, Guangdong Province, China

Designed by Stephanie Strouse

DOM Aug 2019, Job # 02-008-01

May your childhood be filled with adventure, your days with hope and your learnings with wisdom, and may you continuously grow as an MVP Kid, preparing to lead a responsible, meaningful life.

—SOPHIA DAY

The Jordan family was on their annual* beach camping trip. They always came during Spring Break for the **kids' sandcastle contest.**

***Annual** means something that is done once a year.

Ezekiel and his siblings, Harmony, Faith and Malik, gathered their sand tools and headed to the beach.

"This year, I'm going to make a castle I can fit into!" exclaimed Faith.

"Mine is going to have a moat!" Ezekiel planned with excitement.

As they gathered in the contest area, Ezekiel looked longingly at this year's grand prize.

"I'd really love to win the SuperKite!" he thought.

Ezekiel chose his building space. Faith and Harmony claimed the spot next to him. Malik didn't like to play with sand, so he searched for small shells, sea glass and driftwood to decorate their castles.

When the lifeguard blew the start whistle, Ezekiel began packing wet sand to create the walls of his castle.

He dug out the moat and used the sand to build guard towers and turrets*.

***Turrets** are small towers attached to a castle.

He cut out stairs and carved windows.

It was the **best** castle he had ever made!

Ezekiel went over to see how his sisters were doing. They were building a dribble castle large enough for Faith to sit inside!
"Wow! Great job!" he said.

"Two more minutes to finish your castles," the lifeguard called out.

"Oh no! I'd better get back to work!"

He ran into the sea
to fill his buckets.

He began pouring water into the moat. He couldn't help but glance up again at the SuperKite prize when...

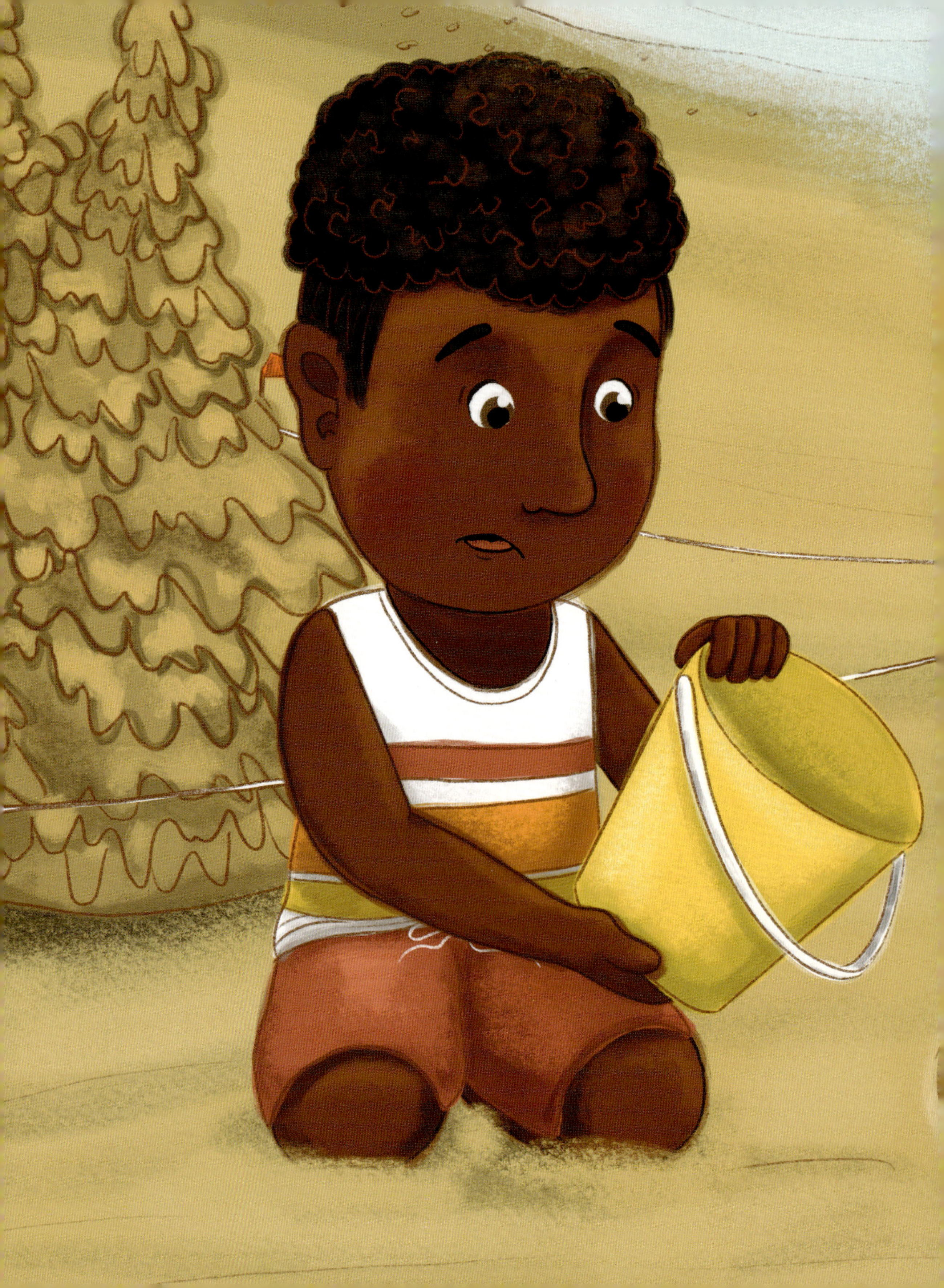

"Oh no! My castle!"

Ezekiel watched his masterpiece dissolve right before his eyes.

Ezekiel picked up the stone that had been the castle door.

"I'll be back at camp," he told his family.

"What a mistake! I can't believe I did that."

While his family enjoyed the campfire, Ezekiel sulked. He was **angry** and **feeling sorry** for himself.

"What a waste of time. I shouldn't have even entered the contest," he said to his dad. "It was worthless."

"Let's take a run," his dad suggested.

Usually both his mind and body felt better after a run. "Okay," he agreed.

"I know you're upset about your castle, Ezekiel, but let's not let it ruin your vacation. Could you find a little good about today?"

"I completely destroyed my castle. There's no good to find in that."

"Everyone makes mistakes sometimes. If you **carry them around,** they **weigh your spirit down.**"

"But I missed my chance to win the SuperKite. I can't stop thinking about it," Ezekiel complained.

"I'm sorry. I know you regret what happened."

"*Re-what?*'" asked Ezekiel.

"Regret. It's feeling sad or angry when you think about how something might have gone differently."

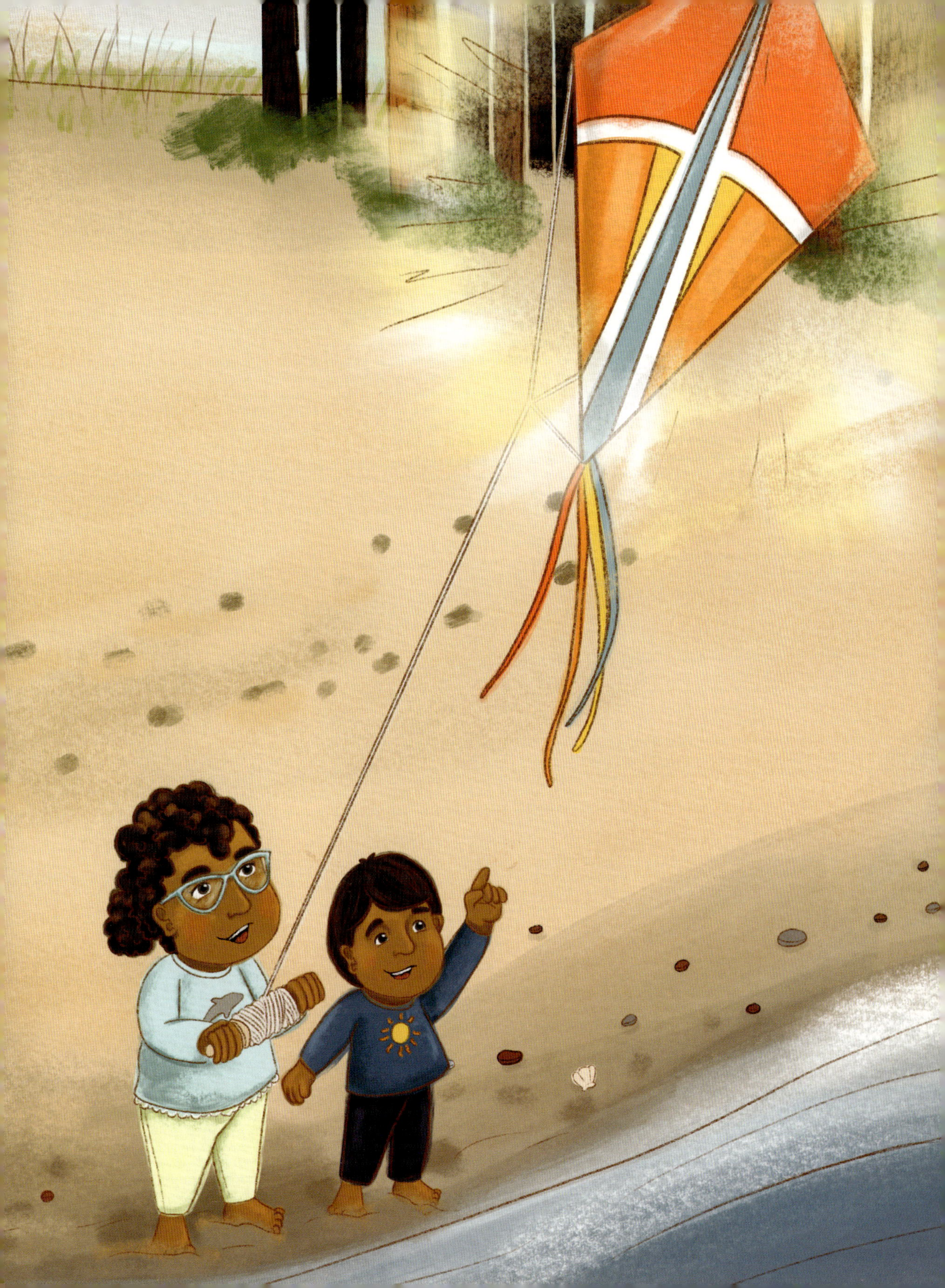

"That pretty much explains how I feel about *everything*," Ezekiel said.

"What do you mean 'everything?'"

Ezekiel's dad had no idea that Ezekiel was always, ALWAYS **over-thinking his mistakes** and **poor choices.**

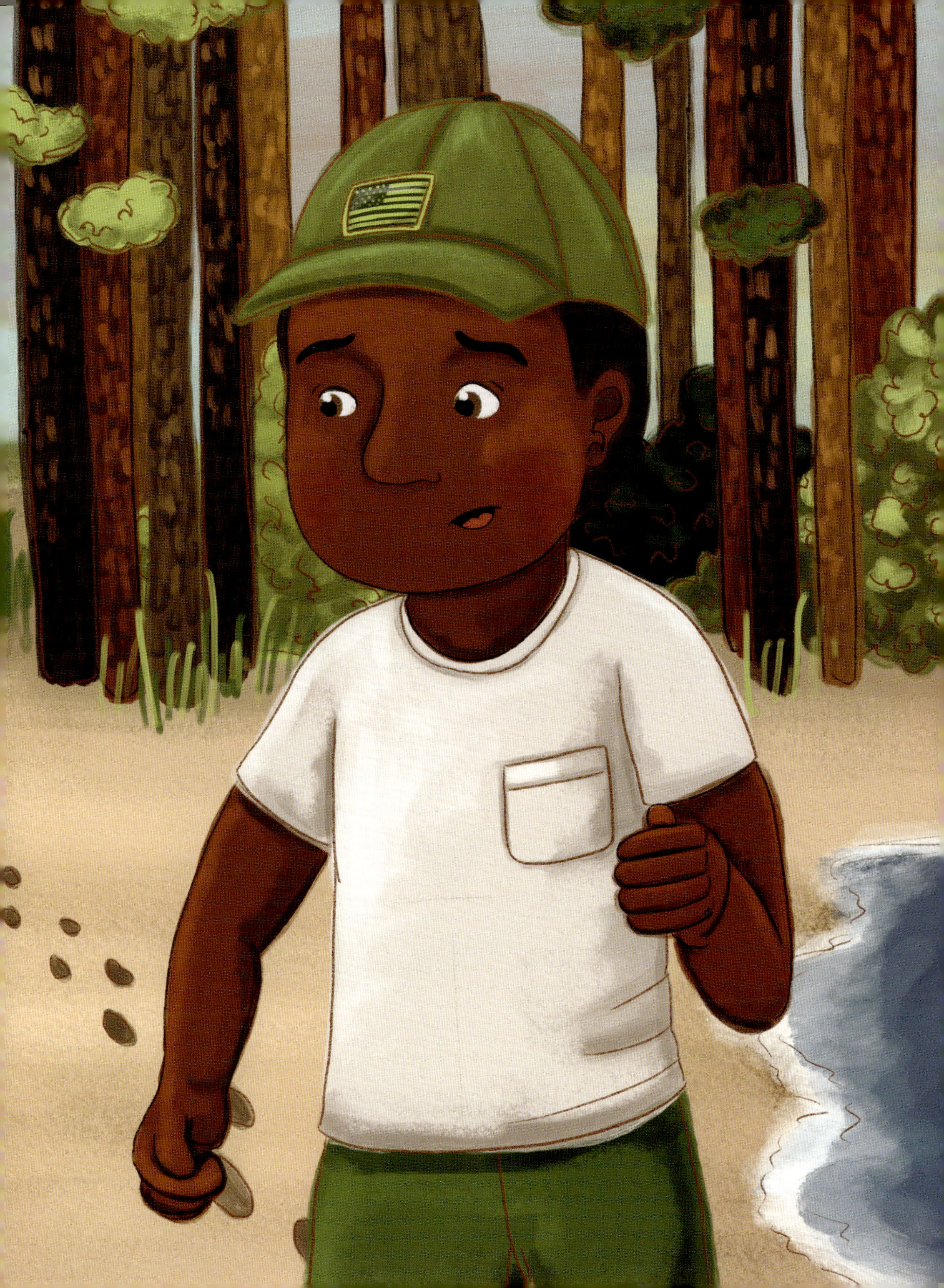

Ezekiel told his dad about all the regrets he was carrying. Some were **recent mistakes** - He was stressed that he didn't finish his homework before vacation. He replayed over and over again the shot he missed at his last basketball game.

Others he had **carried for a long time** - He regretted a friendship he lost over a silly argument. He would be sad forever about not going to visit his grandfather when he was sick.

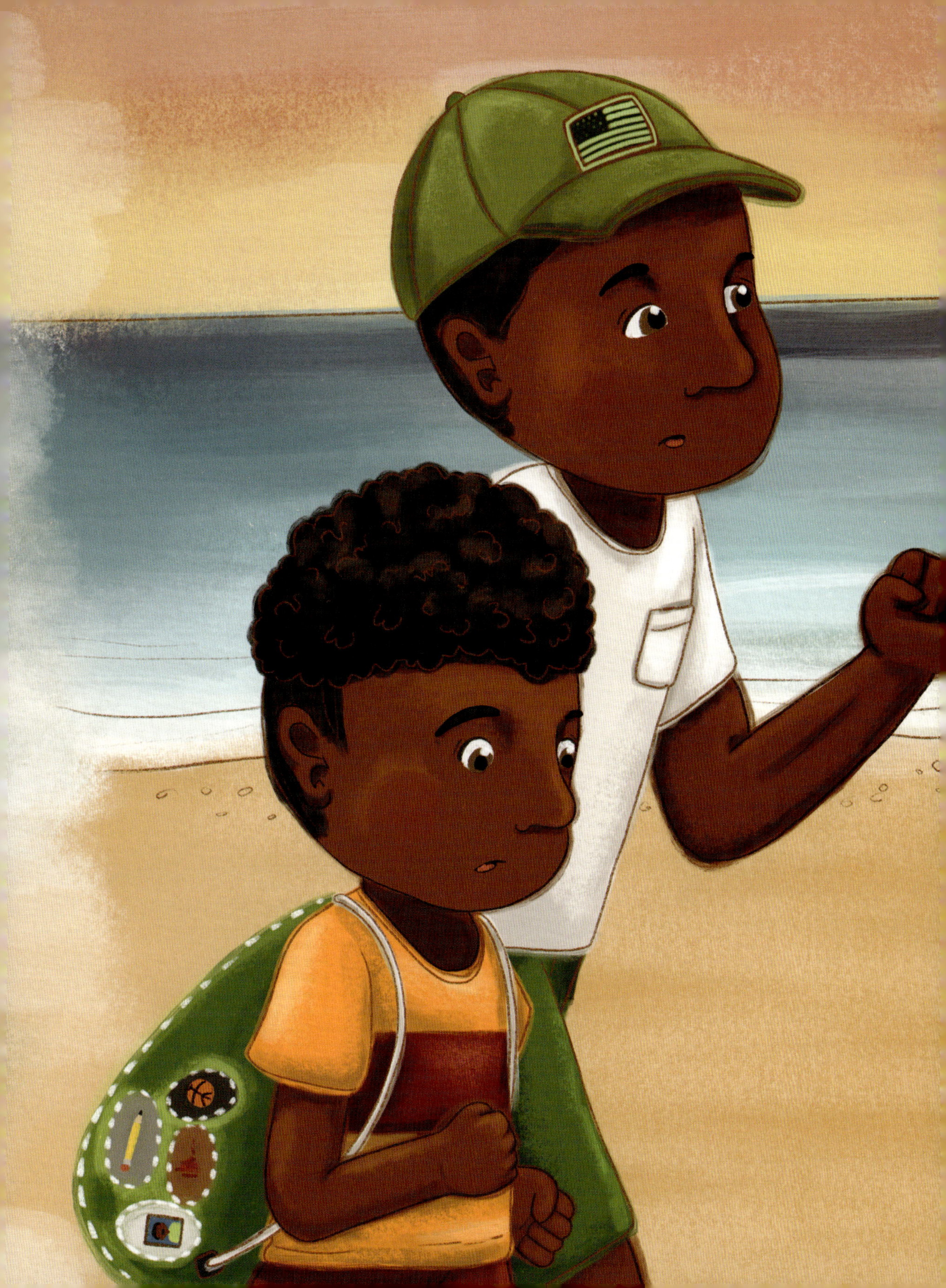

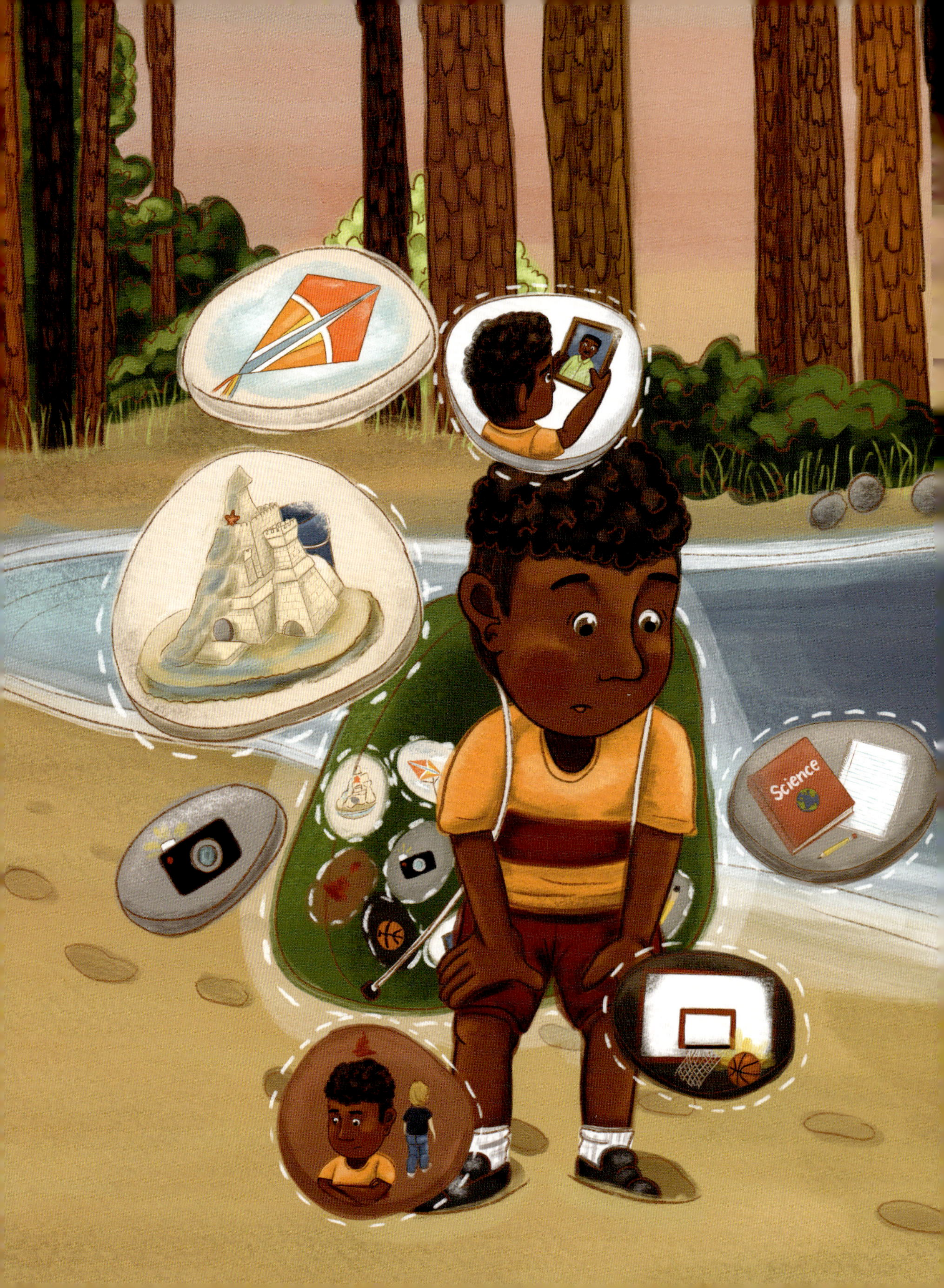
Science

Ezekiel wondered if he might have won the sandcastle contest if he hadn't tried the moat. He could be flying his SuperKite right now.

"Dad! I didn't even get a picture of my castle! It was the best one I've ever built."

Ezekiel was sinking into despair.

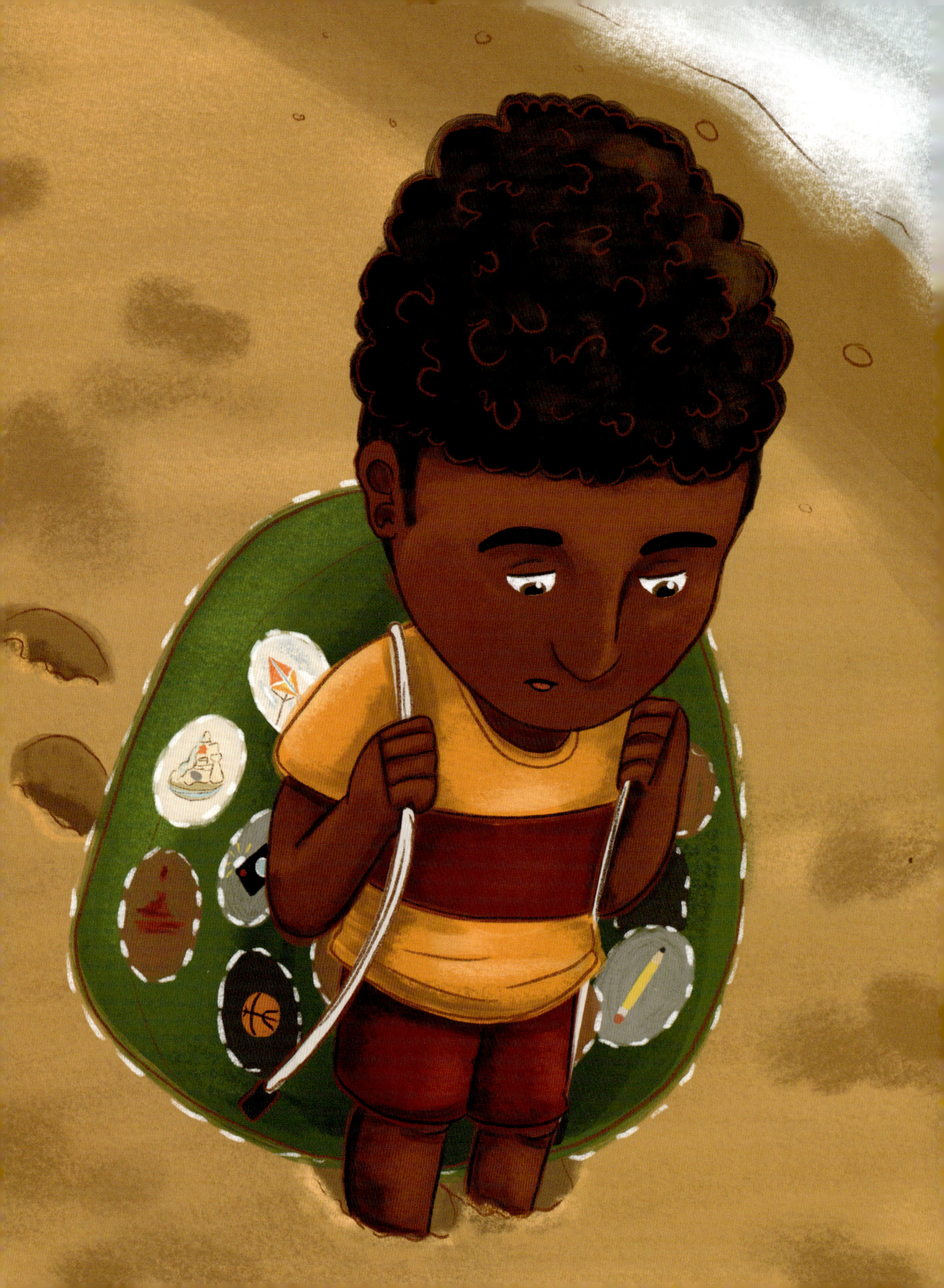

"That's a lot to carry, son.
It isn't bad to feel regret. It shows that you know your choice wasn't the best one. That's powerful knowledge, and it can either make you weaker or stronger. The important thing is what you do with your regret."

"I wish I could just wash it all away," Ezekiel said, "forget it ever happened."

"Well, we can't wash away the past, but we can lay it down."

"How do I lay it down?'"

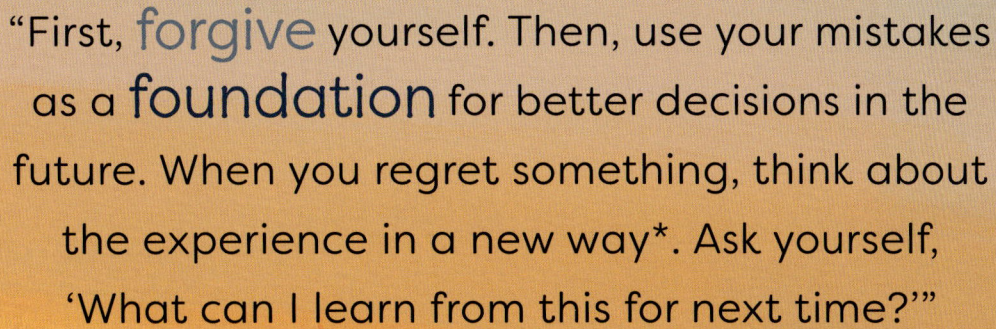

"First, forgive yourself. Then, use your mistakes as a foundation for better decisions in the future. When you regret something, think about the experience in a new way*. Ask yourself, 'What can I learn from this for next time?'"

*Thinking about something in a new way, or turning a negative thought into a positive one, is called **"reframing."**

Ezekiel thought for a moment. "Next time I won't build a moat."

"You were excited about that moat!
"Don't let regret turn into fear of trying hard things.
Look for the wisdom. Stop and think.
What really destroyed your castle?"

"I lost my focus and poured the water too quickly."
Suddenly, Ezekiel remembered something
about water damage in his unfinished
science homework.

"Dad! If I had finished my homework, I might not have made that mistake! Let's rebuild the castle tomorrow. I can **find my mistake** and **do it right** next time."

While his siblings roasted s'mores by the fire, Ezekiel finished his homework. He was missing out, but he was sure **he wouldn't regret this choice.**

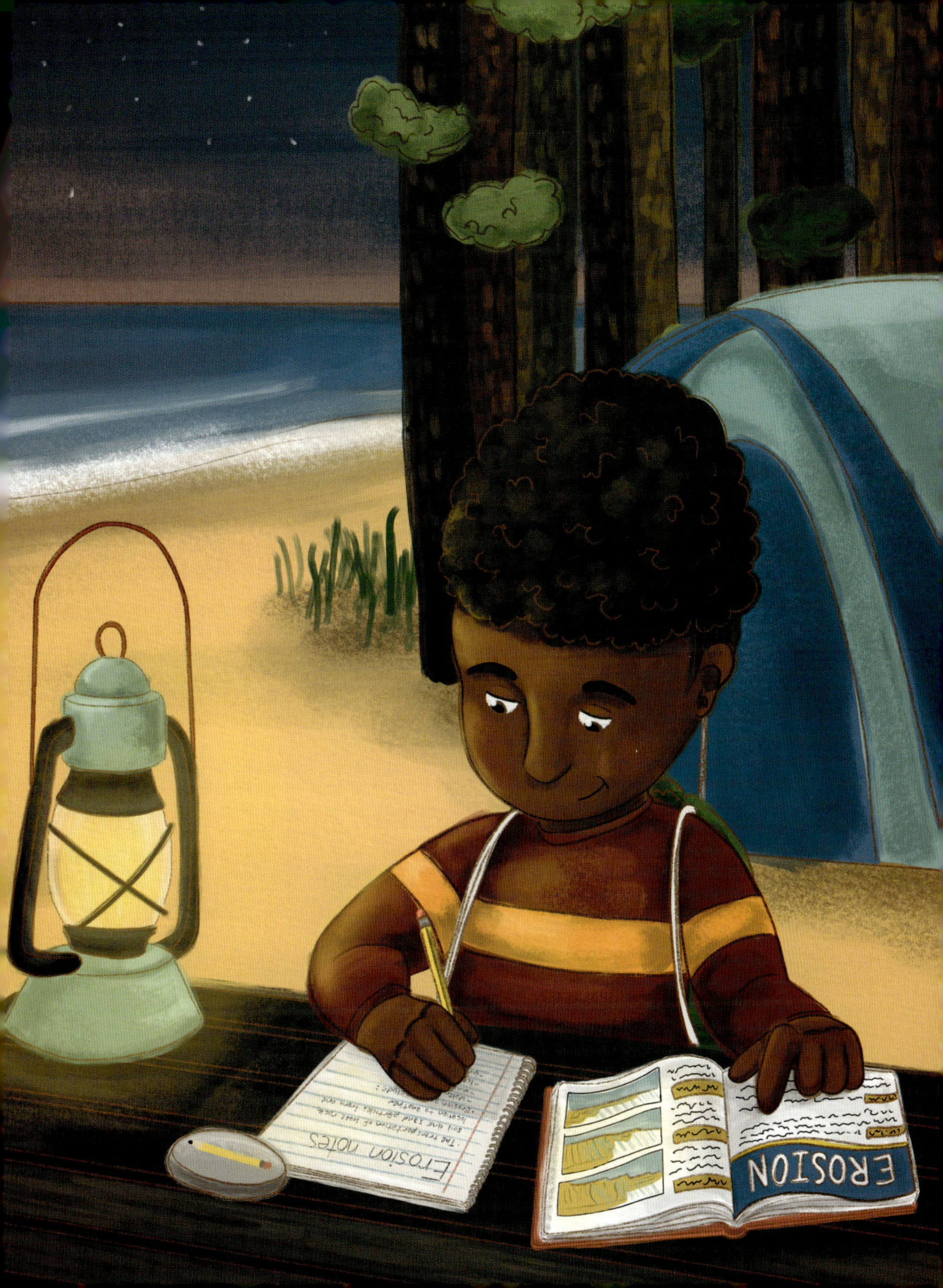
Erosion notes
EROSION

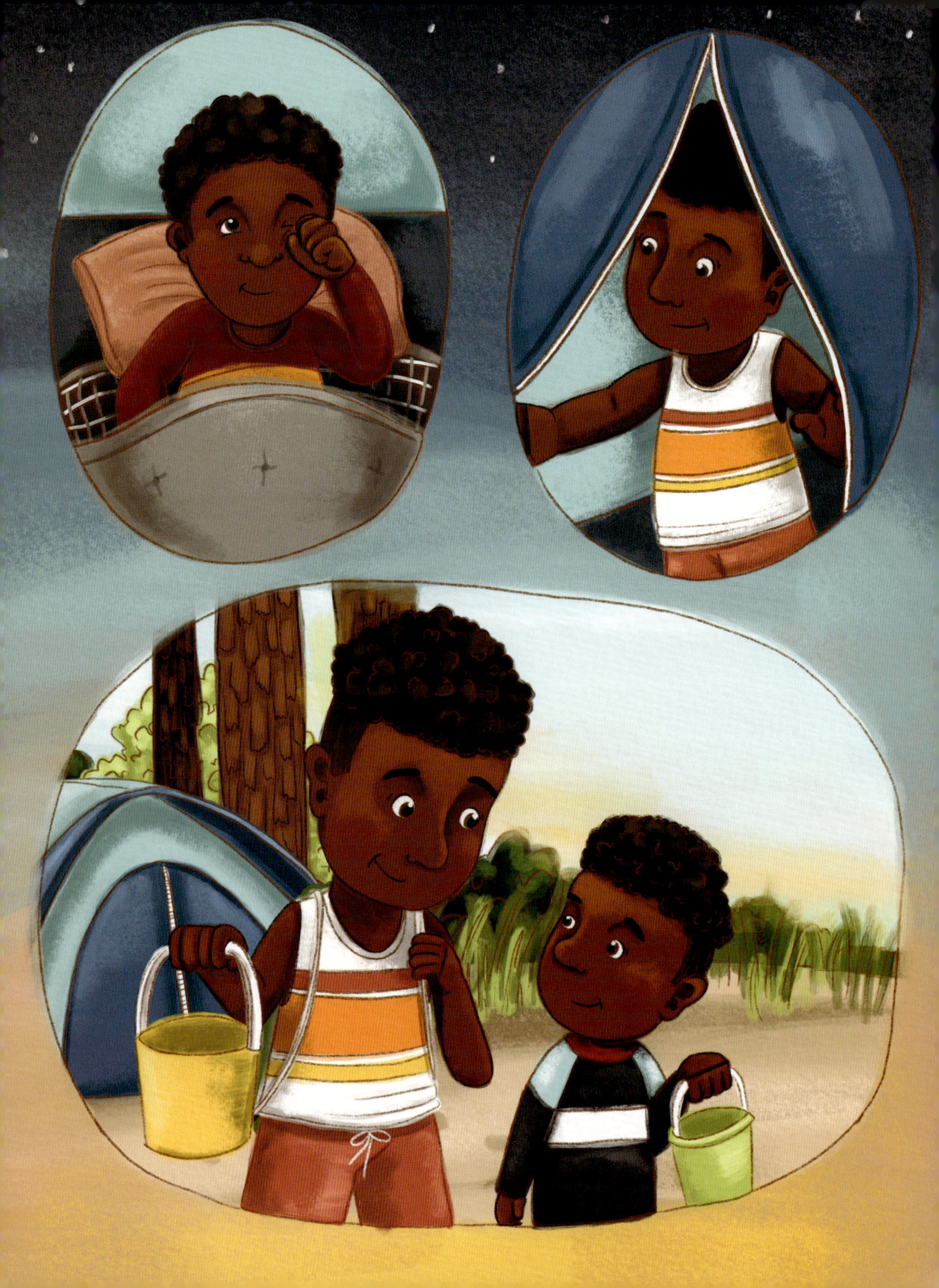

In the morning, Ezekiel gathered his sandcastle supplies. He enlisted Malik to help him gather stones.

As he pressed the stones into the sand, he thought about the **regrets** he was **carrying**. How could he use them to **build a strong foundation** for the future?

"Next time, I'll pass the ball if I don't have a clear shot.

I'll apologize to my friend and not be so careless with my words again.

From now on, I'll take every opportunity to show people I love them."

Ezekiel built on top of the stone foundation.
He began packing wet sand to create
the walls of his castle.

He dug out the moat and used the sand
to build guard towers and turrets.
He cut out stairs and carved windows.

All that was left was to fill the moat.
"This time, I'll protect it from erosion."

He learned from his science homework that erosion*
happens when there isn't enough other stuff in the
soil to keep it in place. He asked Malik and his sisters
to help him gather seaweed and shells.

***Erosion** is the process of soil being worn away by wind or water.

They pressed their findings into the walls of the moat.

He had **learned from experience** that fast-flowing water causes quick erosion. His homework said that slow-flowing water takes more time to cause damage.

He slowly – *very slowly* – poured a bucket of water into the moat.

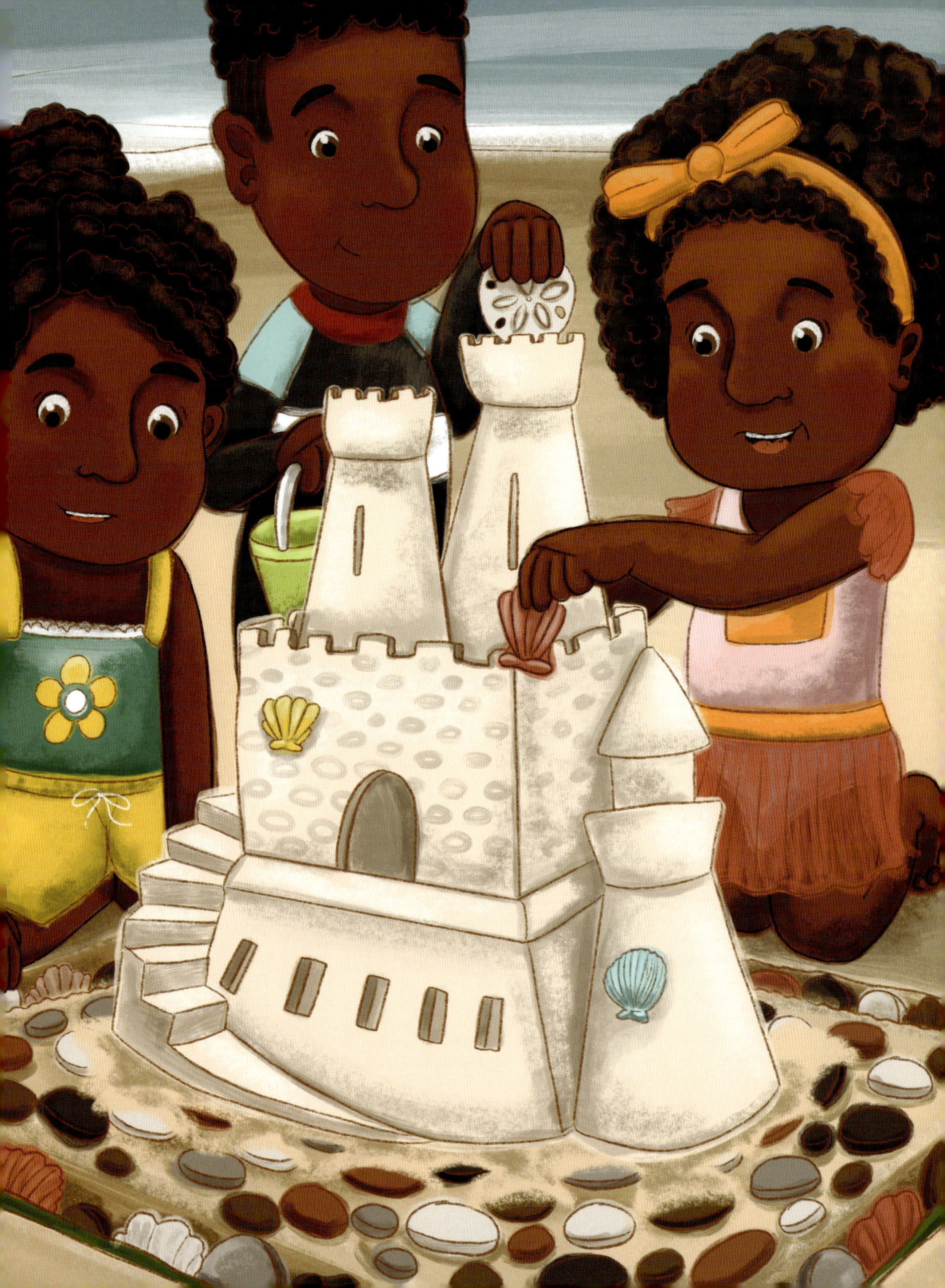

It worked! They had kept the water from washing away the castle.

"Now THIS one really is our best castle yet!"

Ezekiel knew he would make many more mistakes in life, but now knew how to **forgive himself** and **use his mistakes to build a foundation** for wiser choices.

YOU'RE A REAL mvpkid!

Remember to finish your homework!
9
17
YOU'RE A REAL mvpkid!
Mistak
are
Stepping
Stones
to success.

The chance I didn't take,
The bad choice that I made,
They collect and find a way
To ruin every day.

What might have happened if...
If only I had done...
It might have gone much better
If only I had known.

Each heavy stone I carry-
The anger, shame, regret,
Mistakes, neglect and failures-
I can't seem to forget.

But I'll be brave. I'll face the pain,
I'll build on my mistakes.
I don't have to hold them tight.
I'll lay down these keepsakes.

What weighed me down in weakness
Became a stone of strength,
A wise and firm foundation
For the next choice I must make.

I won't give up! These hopes of mine
Won't be washed out to sea.
Now I know, for next time,
What I'll do differently.

LEARN & DISCUSS

Ezekiel is learning to understand and handle his regrets. Learn with Ezekiel and discuss how you can learn from mistakes and lay down regret, too!

> I was having a great time at the sandcastle contest until I accidentally ruined my castle. I had hoped I would win the prize.

Describe how Ezekiel felt when his sandcastle dissolved. Have you ever felt this way?

> Once I started talking with my dad about my regrets, I realized I had a lot! People tend to avoid thinking about regrets because it can cause sadness, anger or other negative feelings. Unfortunately, sometimes pain has to be part of the healing process.

Is there anything you need to talk about with someone? Who do you trust to listen to you or give you wise advice?

> I regretted that I missed the opportunity to visit my grandfather when he was sick. Sometimes the things people regret the most are things they didn't do.

Is there anything you decided NOT to do that you now regret? What will you do the next time you have a similar opportunity?

> One of my regrets was a friendship I lost because I said something unkind.

Do you regret anything you've said to someone?

How can you restore your relationship?

> Throughout the story, I carry a sack of rocks. This represents the heavy feeling of sadness or regret about my mistakes. Before I learned to use mistakes to build a better future, they just felt like a weight to carry. Now, I know mistakes can be used as a tool.

If the way you feel right now were a sack full of something, what would be inside?

Every feeling has a purpose. What do you think is the best way to use your feelings right now?

> I learned that wishing things had turned out differently isn't helpful. It only keeps me stuck feeling badly about myself. I can turn a bad experience into something good, though! If I learn from it, even a bad experience can help me make better choices in the future.

What is one good thing that you have learned from bad experiences?

Think about a good decision you made. How did you learn the wisdom to make that good decision?

> I had the opportunity to rebuild my sandcastle using stones to strengthen the foundation, and it worked! This is a good example of how we can learn from our mistakes to make better choices.

Have you had a chance to re-do something in a better way?

How does it feel to use what you learned from a previous mistake?

How can you help your child lay down regret?

Respond with compassion. The most important factor in your child's response to their mistakes is your own response. Before reacting, take a deep breath and remind yourself to respond with compassion rather than scolding. Children need to feel they can safely make mistakes without losing your love. Only after sharing compassion, talk to the child about alternate outcomes for different choices. For example: I'm sorry you're so tired. If you had gone to bed on time last night instead of playing, you wouldn't be too tired to go to your friend's house after school today.

Practice thoughtful questions. Teaching children how to think about their own thought patterns is an important part of developing a growth mindset. When your child is wrestling with big thoughts and feelings, try asking open-ended questions.

Find out about their motivations by asking questions such as:
Can you tell me more about why you think that?
Why did you choose to do it that way?

Help a child consider alternate outcomes with questions like:
What might have been different if you had followed directions?
Would it be different if you had asked for help?

Some questions can help kids think through solutions, such as:
How will you do that differently next time?
What good things did you learn from this experience?

Encourage literary analysis. With younger children, introduce these questions while reading picture books together: "What is the character thinking right now? Which choice would you make? What might happen if the character makes that choice?"

Learn from past moments of regret. Whenever possible, allow your child to revisit an experience that has caused regret. Even if the actual event cannot be recreated, the opportunity to practice a new thought pattern and to quickly put into practice the wisdom gained by an experience will free children from negative feelings. This will solidify their belief in their own abilities to choose a better option. Although Ezekiel could not re-do the contest, rebuilding his castle gave him concrete assurance in his ability and he will be less likely to continue to ruminate on failure.

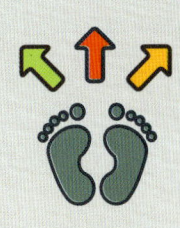

Learning and practicing forethought. The ultimate goal in teaching kids to learn from their failures and to build on mistakes is to prevent repeating the same mistakes through forethought, thinking before acting. With enough practice and when the child is developmentally ready, the question of "how would it have been different?" becomes "what might happen if I do this?" Thinking through the possible outcomes of various options before making a choice is the result of lots of trial and error.

Mistakes can show positive risk-taking. Help your children realize that making a mistake is proof that they are taking risks and learning something new. No one can avoid mistakes altogether, but the more we learn from them, the better we can minimize their negative impact in our lives.

For additional tip and reference information, visit www.mvpkids.com.

Meet the

mvpkids®

featured in
Ezekiel Builds on his Mistakes™

EZEKIEL JORDAN

FAITH JORDAN

Can you also find this MVP Kid®?

FRANKIE RUSSO

Also featuring...

MR. DARIUS JORDAN
"Dad"

MRS. JASMINE JORDAN
"Mom"

HARMONY JORDAN
Sister

MALIK JORDAN
Brother

Grow up with our MVPkids

CELEBRATE!™ Board Books
Ages 0-6

Our **CELEBRATE**™ board books for toddlers and preschoolers focus on social, emotional, educational and physical needs. Helpful Teaching Tips are included in each book to equip parents to guide their children deeper into the subject of the book.

help me BECOME™
Early Elementary
Ages 4-10

Our **Help Me Become**™ series for early elementary readers tells three short stories in each book of our MVP Kids® inspiring character growth. Each story concludes with a discussion guide to help the child process the story and apply the concepts.

STOP BULLYING

Don't miss out on our 3-part **STAND** anti-bullying series!

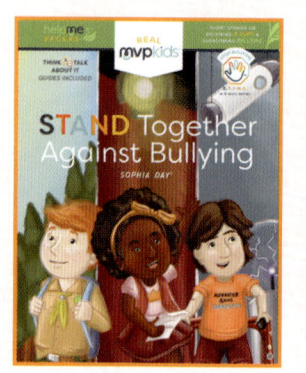

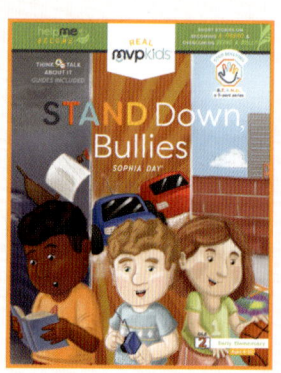

help me UNDERSTAND™ Elementary
Ages 6-12

Help your children grow in understanding emotions by collecting the entire **Help Me Understand**™ series!

Our **Help Me Understand**™ series for elementary readers shares the stories of our MVP Kids® learning to understand and manage a specific emotion. Readers will gain tools to take responsibility for their own emotions and develop healthy relationships.

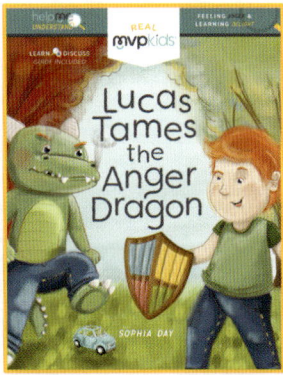

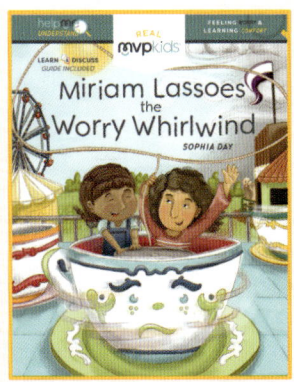

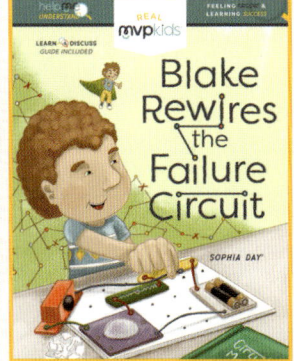

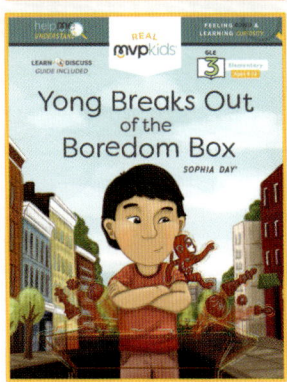

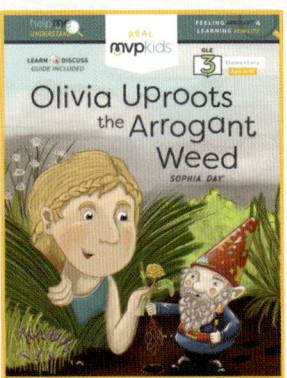

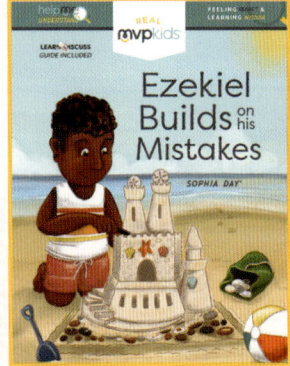

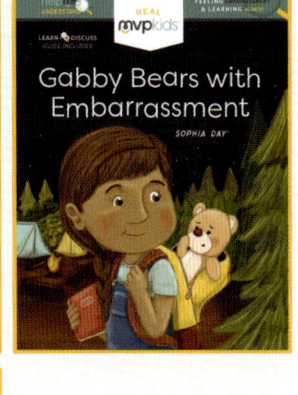

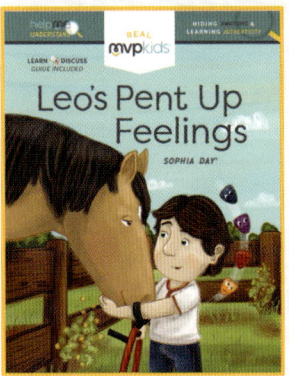

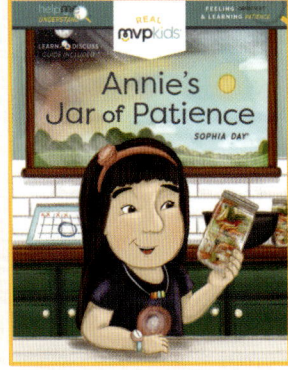

- Lucas Tames the Anger Dragon
- Miriam Lassoes the Worry Whirlwind
- Blake Rewires the Failure Circuit
- Sarah Sizes Up the Insecure Ant
- Yong Breaks Out of the Boredom Box
- Olivia Uproots the Arrogant Weed
- Ezekiel Builds on his Mistakes
- Gabby Bears with Embarrassment
- Leo's Pent Up Feelings
- Annie's Jar of Patience

www.mvpkids.com

JUL 02 2019

YONG CHEN

LEO RUSSO

FRANKIE RUSSO

JULIA ROJAS

GABBY GONZALEZ

AANYA PATEL

ANNIE JAMES

BLAKE JAMES

SARAH COHEN-GOLDSTEIN